"If there's a book that truly captures the magic of falling in love with New York, this is the one. Ria Sim's beautiful and whimsical sensibility oozes through every page. It feels like having your best friend by your side, guiding you through every season of life."
—GRACE KANG, owner of Pink Olive

"Ria Sim's colorful and personal work guides us through cafes, stores, and street scenes to unexpected corners of beauty—a birdhouse on Grove Street, a cellist on West 4th— amid the city's hard edifices of steel, stone, and ambition. Her vision is a gift to all who dwell here (or aspire to)!"
—JOHN DONAHUE, author of *All the Restaurants* and @eat.draw.repeat

"[Ria Sim's] point of view of local spots in New York City is unparalleled in her level of detail. By far one of my favorite artists!"
—ALEX LAROSA, founder of LaRosa Bakery

"Ria Sim is such a bright light. Her positivity and love for New York are evident on every page of her book. She inspires me to stop and take the time to appreciate this magical city we're so lucky to live in."
—KERRY DIAMOND, cofounder and editorial director at Cherry Bombe

"Ria Sim has a Rumpelstiltskin-like ability to spin the fleece of ordinary life into gold."
—BRANDON BORROR-CHAPPELL and LAURA BROWN

Dear New York,
I Love You

Dear New York, I Love You

An Artist's Celebration of the City

RIA SIM

Countryman Press

An Imprint of W. W. Norton & Company
Independent Publishers Since 1923

Copyright © 2025 by Ria Sim

For information about permission to reproduce selections from this book, write to
Permissions, Countryman Press, 500 Fifth Avenue, New York, NY 10110

For information about special discounts for bulk purchases, please contact
W. W. Norton Special Sales at specialsales@wwnorton.com or 800-233-4830

Manufacturing by Toppan Leefung
Book design by Allison Chi
Production manager: Devon Zahn

Countryman Press
www.countrymanpress.com

An imprint of W. W. Norton & Company, Inc.
500 Fifth Avenue, New York, NY 10110
www.wwnorton.com

978-1-68268-908-0

1 2 3 4 5 6 7 8 9 0

This book is dedicated to my dear grandfather, who sacrificed to come to America to give his grandchildren the privilege of being American citizens and a chance at a better tomorrow.

And to my boys . . .
Thank you from the bottom of my heart for the precious gift of being your mom. May every day inspire you from the moment you step outside, and may you always have the courage to be the architects of your own tomorrows. You are my greatest treasures, and I believe in the magic you will create!

Contents

Dear New York,

Just a little note from me to you, a heartfelt thank-you for wrapping me in your love. It's incredible how you welcomed me with open arms into your vibrant embrace. Every day as I stroll along your streets, absorb the bustling city symphony, witness the remarkable beauty you generously share, and catch the scent of each new season's beginning, my heart overflows with joy! Who would have thought you could fill me with so much happiness?

You've been my source of hope, new beginnings, and a treasure trove of memories. In your magical presence, I've glimpsed meaningful moments from my past. It might be magic or just a beautiful coincidence, but you and I both know that the gifts you offer are tailor-made for each of us. The real trick is for us to notice these gifts.

Thank you for taking my hand and pulling me out of my apartment to be with you on a daily basis. The blooming springs, the warm summer evenings casting a golden glow, the vibrant leaves dancing in the fall, and the soft evening lights reflecting off snow-covered streets in January–I hold them all close to my heart with deep gratitude.

May you continue to shine brightly through every season, sharing your incredible beauty and offering endless canvases to illustrate.

With love and gratitude,
Ria

Introduction

For the longest time, I suspected that New York City was my soulmate.

You know that feeling when you lay eyes on New York for the first time? It's like a whirlwind of wonder, a surge of excitement, almost as if you can feel the city's vibrant energy flowing through your veins. Whether you're soaring in on an airplane, crossing a majestic bridge over the East or Hudson River, or just catching a glimpse of the iconic skyline on a movie screen—it's a moment of magic. Your heart races, your chest swells, and you realize that you're falling in love with New York.

It's mesmerizing. For me, it was love at first sight. Okay, maybe it started out as a crush: I admired the city from afar, since I grew up 2,500 miles away on the West Coast. No matter where you are in the world, you've heard tales of New York. There's this inexplicable connection, even if you've never set foot in the city. It's a blend of the familiar and the unknown, all wrapped up in a single moment. From the countless stories told through movies, books, photographs, paintings, and commercials, there's a sense of longing and connection and *possibility*. My family (my grandparents, parents, older sister, and I) immigrated to the United States—from China, via Indonesia—when I was just five years old. As a child, I used to sit with my grandfather every New Year's Eve and watch the ball drop in Times Square on his tiny TV. I would see images of New York in the fashion magazines I loved to read, on countless TV shows, and in my favorite movies.

I first visited New York City as an adult and the city was like this massive magnet, pulling me closer with every visit, inviting me to dive into its vast sea of creativity. I was living in the Bay Area, running a floral and events boutique I'd founded, when an unexpected turn of events changed my path forever. I was diagnosed with an autoimmune illness and had to close my business to focus on healing and recovery. As part of my healing, I began drawing and posting my illustrations on this new outlet my oldest son introduced me to: Instagram. When I created my account, @coffeecakescafe, I started out sharing doodles expressing my love for coffee. Completely self-taught, I illustrated details and scenes from my favorite Bay Area cafes, just hoping to bring attention to some of my favorite spots and a smile to anyone who saw my art. But my heart was still in New York City . . .

As the years of drawing unfolded, so did my curiosity about New York. I began visiting the city regularly, and during those visits, I drew the city as a way to play make-believe, to live in my little reality. After a challenging upbringing, I mostly lived my life in a make-believe world just to keep going. I would take lots of photos of what I saw in New York—cute cafe facades, independent boutiques, pretty gardens, stately townhouses. Back home in California, I would create illustrations from my photos, enhancing the reality captured in them with *my* reality. When I start drawing, I see the picture as it is–the imperfections of the building, the unkempt streets, the broken sidewalks, and the piling trash. But I also see the beauty that New York offers. So I add a flower-pot in front of a shop, a hanging plant, a bicycle with a basket of flowers, or some other whimsical element to express the joy and wonder I feel for the city.

Eventually, my dream came true, and I moved to New York City! Before I moved here, I didn't know much about the different neighbor-hoods. It took a while before I discovered the five boroughs, each still waiting for my further exploration. I've learned to take life one step at a time, focusing more on the present moment than the relentless pursuit of what comes next. For years, life was a climb to make it to some-where, and now I found that all along that "somewhere" was right here, in New York.

New York City is a treasure trove of history, and here I am, still with so much to learn and explore. I'm still discovering the hidden stories, charms, and mysteries of this urban oasis. Initially overwhelmed with the desire to see everything, I soon realized that wasn't the New York I wanted. I wanted to "feel" New York with my heart and soul.

And now that I live here, I love it every bit as much as I did when I just fantasized about it—and then some. Yes, I get stuck in standstill traffic, deal with subway debacles, and opt to walk even if it means an extra hour. But as I navigate the city's never-ending rhythm, I've discovered that you can live here and still savor a slower pace. I love the hustle and bustle, the honks, horns, sirens, and construction bangs. I love walking at the New Yorker's quick pace. But here's the thing: You can truly relish the serene side of life here as well, if you take the time to appreciate it. The city offers an abundance of parks tucked away in each neighborhood, along with infinite numbers of cafes and benches and hidden spots, inviting you to sit and enjoy watching New Yorkers come and go.

Writing a book about the city I adore with all my heart adds another layer to the excitement. I'm so moved by this moment in my life. How lucky am I to be given this opportunity. How fortunate I am to start a new chapter in my life at this age. And how thankful I am to be able to see the world through the eyes of a child. I see New York with my heart. In my heart, I see its magic, its beauty. In this book, I want people to feel invited, as if they are walking with me to see my favorite places.

This book is my little journey of discovering the city I love through all four seasons. Each season plays a special tune in my heart—not a specific song, but continuous melodies of happiness, excitement, and new discoveries throughout the year. This book is an invitation to journey with me through a year here, noticing how the city changes with the seasons, one discovery at a time. Come, take my hand, and explore it with me!

SPRING

A burst of joy that's impossible to contain!

Dear Spring,

How can I even begin to describe the magic of spring in the Big Apple? It's like a breath of fresh air after a long, chilly winter. And after months of shivering under cozy blankets and gazing longingly out the window, my hands pressed to the glass, I ask to no one in particular, "Is it spring yet?"

The weather, oh, it's just right—not too hot, not too cold, like Goldilocks's porridge. We shed our heavy winter coats and scarves, and we can finally bid farewell to those clunky boots. It's time to slip on our sneakers and take a leisurely walk through Central Park, or any of the charming neighborhood parks scattered across the city. And, of course, the pretty floral dresses popping up in shops are impossible to resist. My fellow ladies, can you relate to that irresistible urge for a couple of new spring dresses (wink-wink, nudge-nudge)? Do you recall the last time you bought a spring dress, put it on, and twirled in the mirror feeling giddy? I get excited to take my dress out for a walk to the park so I can see it sway from side to side as I walk, while I check out the trees to see if there are new buds waiting to sprout.

Speaking of parks, Central Park in spring is an absolute marvel. The flowers burst into a rainbow of colors, and the park is filled with laughter and music. It's a place where you can simply unwind, leaving behind the thoughts swirling in your head. It's an escape from the hustle and bustle of reality.

One of my favorite springtime activities is strolling through my neighborhood to listen to my feathered friends. Yes, I may sound a bit silly calling them friends, but they are! I adore hearing their cheerful chirps, and sometimes it seems like they're having animated conversations too. I can't help but wonder what the topic of their conversation might be: Is it bickering about who will get dinner, or perhaps one is explaining the handyman repairs that need to be made on the nest? Or maybe they're complaining about the loud construction noise across the street (I had to sneak that one in, with a wink). The chirps also remind me of listening to the old-fashioned typewriter that kept my grandfather company. He'd type letters every day to family and friends. So, instead of hearing all the bird noise as irritating, it's actually soothing to me because I picture him safe at home, sitting at the kitchen table, sending hugs to loved ones.

Now, let's talk about the cherry blossoms—these delicate trees that grace the city with their elegance and beauty and tug at my heartstrings. It's as if I step outside and the city greets me with a sea of pink and white. As cherry blossoms are so short-lived, I make sure I walk every day to capture as many as I can before they start to fade in the wind. If there's a breeze, I see the petals float in the air at Waverly Place. I stand on the corner and just watch them dance in the gentle wind and you know secretly I'm dancing too.

Springtime in New York wouldn't be complete without the promise of one thing: ice cream! You can find ice cream in every nook and cranny of the city. I often hear the familiar jingle of the ice cream truck from inside my apartment. Each time I hear it, it takes me back in time to my childhood, a delightful feeling of nostalgia. I remember a time when I was about seven years old and my grandpa gave me a handful of change to get us both an ice cream. I excitedly skipped down the street toward the music (while he of course lagged at his usual turtle pace). I picked the ice cream sandwich, and I was happy my grandpa did too. I handed the coins over to the ice cream man in his white suit, and my grandpa opened the wrapper for me. Moments later, as we walked back to the house, I realized I was eating my last bite and saw that my grandpa hadn't touched his yet and so I asked him why. He said with a loving grin, "I'm bringing it back for your grandma. She likes ice cream sandwiches too." I smiled, but you know what I was thinking, right?! *Can I have a bite?* Memories like this, when they suddenly sweep over you, are true treasures. I can't help but be amazed at the many warm recollections I experience just by being in this city.

Spring in New York is like a fresh start, a chance to hit the reset button. It's a time of hope and renewal, a reminder that no matter how tough things may seem, brighter, sunnier days are on the horizon. So, my dear friends, if you ever find yourself in the heart of New York City in the spring, embrace the enchantment of the season. It's a time when the city itself seems to awaken, almost like the magic of a first kiss. Yes, I'm a hopeless romantic, and I hold those memories dear, even if there aren't that many!

Oh, how delightful it is to share some charming spots that have a special place in my heart! Let me whisk you away to these enchanting places . . .

Nat's on Bank, 51 Bank Street

Cafe Cluny, 284 West 12th Street

A true West 12th staple adored by many. It never fails to satisfy my comfort cravings, especially with their perfectly crafted tuna burgers. The picturesque location steals my heart and, regardless of the season, their outdoor seating is my sanctuary. Last Halloween, I secured a front-row seat at 5:30 p.m., relishing my favorite tuna burger while watching the charming parade of kiddies, both young and old, in their costumes. What a treat!

Myers of Keswick, 634 Hudson Street
Opposite: Casa Magazines, 22 8th Avenue

114 Waverly Place

The historic Waverly Place home is a piece of history that once blushed in pink. Every visit to the city demands a photo of this historic home, now transformed into a magnificent haven by the Novogratz family. The golden-yellow smile it radiates warms my heart like the morning sun, embodying the love and history that reside within its walls.

Garber Hardware, 207A 9th Street

Garber Hardware at 207A 9th Avenue is a neighborhood hardware store wrapped in layers of history and
kindness. Imagine stepping into a place that's been
around since 1884! My first visit was initially just
popping in for spare keys, painters' tape, and a box
cutter. But then the magic happened when I found
myself lost for a good half hour wandering through
the aisles. Hardware stores, you see, have always
been a craft shop for big people in my eyes, a senti-
ment I inherited from those cherished trips with my
dad. And to this day, the aroma of a hardware store
brings back the sweetest memories.

Bonberi Mart, 321 West 11th Street
Opposite: Joe's Pizza, 7 Carmine Street

Kerber's Farm, 264 Bleecker Street

For a taste of Long Island on Bleecker Street, there's Kerber's Farm at 264 Bleecker Street. Long Island came to Manhattan, and I've been hooked ever since! The Kerry Berry pies are a delight, and don't even get me started on the savory hand pies. Stepping into the shop instantly transports you from the West Village to Long Island, and it's a journey I happily take.

Sogno Toscano, 17 Perry Street

On 17 Perry Street, there's Sogno Toscano, a place that stole my heart one fine spring day. Their sandwiches are downright incredible, creating a crazy addicting experience like nothing I've tasted before. The atmosphere is always buzzing with happiness, making it the perfect spot to meet friends, share a meal with loved ones, or enjoy a quiet lunch with yourself.

Spongies Cafe, 121 Baxter Street

From Lucie, 263 East 10th Street

From Lucie at 263 East 10th Street is a bakery that's become the sweetheart of the East Village. Dainty cakes adorned with fresh-cut flowers add an elegant touch (and made it instantly famous when it opened). Featured in magazines, television shows, and collaborating with sought-after brands, From Lucie has woven itself into the fabric of the neighborhood, spreading joy with every delightful treat.

Bar Pisellino, 52 Grove Street

One of the sweetest things I'm discovering, bit by bit, is the chance to make friends in unexpected moments or places.

Meeting Richard and Michael, the creators behind the birdhouses on Grove Street, was a heartwarming moment. As I was writing this book, I wanted so badly to include these charming birdhouses. I've taken countless pictures of them and made excuses to walk through Grove Street just to look at them. This desire led me to meet the two creatives. The moment I met them at their apartment on Grove, we had an instant connection.

They welcomed me with such kindness, and meeting them for tea felt like opening a book filled with treasures. Richard, an actor, director, and producer, and Michael, an interior designer and author, introduced me to their love of the Village and community. Richard has lived in the Village for 50 years, Michael for 25. They've been married for 25 years and have played a crucial role in making Grove Street the charming place it is today. Richard shared that he had a dream to add beauty to the lane by installing red birdhouses in the trees along the way.

When winter comes and the trees are bare, the birdhouses add a pop of color to make residents and passersby smile. From installing the first birdhouse in 2017 to being involved in planting, trimming, or replacing trees, to repairing the wickets that adorn the street, Richard and Michael are heavily involved in several community organizations. They are two gems that sparkle and bring joy to so many in the community. These are moments I treasure: Meeting genuinely kindhearted citizens and hearing their stories reminds me that everyone has a story to tell and taking time to listen leads to new discoveries.

Grove Street

Madame Matovu, 240 West 10th Street
Opposite: Pink Olive, 30 Charles Street

Lingua Franca, 95 Jane Street

I love Lingua Franca at 95 Jane Street. Their sweaters look so cozy; the embroidery is so fun and expressive. Each time I walk by this shop I can't help but stop and peek through the window with eyes of delight!

Boyar Gifts, 388 Bleecker Street
Opposite: Abingdon Square, Hudson Street at 8th Avenue and West 12th Street

Eli's Flowers at Eli's Market, 1411 3rd Avenue

Opposite: Zabar's, 2245 Broadway

Visiting Zabar's at 2245 Broadway and Eli Zabar's Market at 1415 3rd Avenue
is always a treasure hunt for all things delectable.

I'm on the subway, heading home with a heart full of happiness! Why, you ask? Well, isn't it obvious? I've got bags full of goodies from both Zabar's and Eli Zabar's Market! It's a mini adventure for me every time I travel to the Upper West and Upper East Side. If I hit one location, you can bet I'm making a pit stop at the other. From downtown, it's a bit of a distance I can't just stroll to and from, so when I do go, it's true excitement.

My subway journey uptown is tinged with anticipation about what treasures I'll bring back. I usually have a list, but inevitably my bag ends up filled with additional and unexpected items. On my ride back downtown, I feel a deep satisfaction, knowing I did splendidly today, snagging exactly what caught my eye! Sure, I might take up a bit more space on the subway, but hey, a girl's gotta do what a girl's gotta do to satisfy a major uptown craving!

75½ Bedford Street

Have you heard about the skinniest home in Greenwich Village? It measures a mere 9½ feet wide, a charming piece of history that I can't help but marvel at every time I pass by.

49

Clinton St. Baking Company, 4 Clinton Street

Opposite: White Horse Tavern, 567 Hudson Street

Let's dive into history at White Horse Tavern on 567 Hudson Street, New York's second-oldest bar, founded in 1880. A neighborhood icon, this tavern has been a haven for artists, poets, authors, and even patron ghosts!

Bánh by Lauren, 42 Market Street
Opposite: Corner of Waverly Place and West 11th Street

SUMMER

It's sizzle time!

Dear Summer,

Now, I'll try not to make this too dramatic, but for someone who's been a California girl all her life, summer in New York is like stepping into a steamy sauna. In the west, we're used to dry heat, not the kind of humidity that greets you here. But summer in New York? It's a whirlwind of emotions.

The sidewalks are almost steaming with heat, and you can spot folks skillfully navigating their way along pathways of shade. They hop from beneath shop awnings to the cool relief of tree-lined streets, out of reach of the sun's harsh ultraviolet light. And if you're lucky, you might just stroll by an open door and catch a delightful blast of icy air-conditioning, a surprise that feels like a gentle kiss from the city.

The parks are an absolute joy, filled with summer enthusiasts reveling in the sun. Friends and family gather for picnics, sunbathing, or simply basking in the warmth of the city. I adore the brightness, the leisurely evening walks, and the chance to linger at a cafe till late as the days stretch on and on. It's also a delight to see the city in a more laid-back, easygoing state, as many New Yorkers head out to the beaches.

Let's not overlook those dramatic summer thunderstorms that love to make an appearance. Trust me, I welcome them with open arms, and I absolutely love strolling in the rain. Just think about it: You're already hot and sweaty, so the rain is like nature's refreshing shower. Slip on your wellies, throw on a cotton dress, and take a leisurely neighborhood walk to savor the rain. It's one of the best parts of summer, and my umbrella gets to stay home!

The city comes alive with summer activities. Local parks always have something going on, from outdoor movies to yoga to arts and crafts. When I get a chance to sit in the park, I like to make it more interesting than just staring at my phone (something we're all frequently guilty of). I love sitting on a bench to just people-watch, waiting for something to catch my eye. Sometimes I play a little game in my mind like "find something pink," and I always end up amazed by how many pink things I then see.

Summer in New York is an adventure, a rollercoaster of highs and lows, unexpected moments, and oodles of character. The heat can become a bit much, especially by August, when the humidity seems to have reached its peak and the subway turns into a sauna within a sauna. There are days when I can't even go out because the heat is way above my ability to tolerate. Just the thought of having to leave my apartment makes me cringe and all I can think about is feeling the sweat dripping on my back . . . *eee ooo* yuck! Sometimes summer in the city feels like a love/hate affair.

But that's all part of the grand adventure, isn't it? Embrace the heat, welcome the surprises, revel in the joys of the city in summertime, and you're bound to create some unforgettable memories.

57

Hello, Sweet Summer!

Oh, how I adore the delightful world of "curb your dog" signs that sprinkle the city! Each one is a unique masterpiece, some so delightfully funny and others grand in their stature. I've found myself captivated, snapping pictures of these quirky gems, creating a mini collection that I can lovingly revisit one day. I wonder if my favorite sign nowadays will still be my favorite then.

St Tropez, 304 West 4th Street
Opposite: Jack's Wife Freda, 226 Lafayette Street

Bakeri, 150 Wythe Avenue, Brooklyn

And no trip to Brooklyn is complete without a stop at Bakeri on 150 Wythe Avenue. Trust me, it's one of the best bakeries in New York! Their squash pies are a divine revelation. I still remember the first heavenly bite that had me hooked—so good that I had to bring some home. It's a true love affair that grows with every visit.

Ovenly, 31 Greenpoint Avenue, Brooklyn
Opposite: Painted Swan, 407 Court Street, Brooklyn

Don Cafe on Columbus Avenue and West 66th Street

This little illustration is a treasure I hold close to my heart. Inspired by Jamie Stelter's Instagram post capturing the adorable scene of siblings deciding on pastries, I knew I had to bring that sweetness to life in a drawing. Coffee fascination and heartwarming moments, all in one delightful cup!

Murray's Bagels at 500 6th Avenue and Jane Street Garden at 36 Jane Street
Opposite: Central Park

Levain Bakery, 167 West 74th Street

Levain Bakery on 167 West 74th Street, is a destination for an otherworldly cookie experience. I practically floated there, each step filled with anticipation. The first bite? An out-of-body experience. The journey from downtown to that cookie, documented in my heart and now shared in my book.

Maman, 239 Centre Street

Maman—oh, what a magical place! Stepping in for the first time felt like a dream. My art inspired by the treats here (seen on the opposite page) was chosen for the Flag Project at Rockefeller Center, a memory I will treasure forever.

Tartine, 253 West 11th Street
Opposite: Coucou French Class, 154 Grand Street

Corner of West 4th and West 11th Street

Peter Lewy, the maestro of melodies in the West Village! As you wander through those charming streets, listen closely for the dulcet tones of Peter's beautiful cello. It's an unexpected encounter with the heartstrings of the city, capturing the attention of admirers and wide-eyed children.

Mary's Fish Camp, 64 Charles Street

Mary's Fish Camp at 64 Charles Street served its last meal on April 26, 2024. This illustration is a tribute to her love and dedication to this neighborhood for over two decades.

PlantShed, 1 Prince Street

Ah, PlantShed at 1 Prince Street, where dreams
intertwine with blooms and coffee aroma. How do I
describe this shop? It's dreamy, beautiful, yummy, and
filled with eye candy. This was my first experience
in a cafe and floral shop combo. My senses were in
overdrive, from the scent of fresh flowers and plants
to the aroma of freshly brewed coffee. There's a
special place in my heart for floral shops, probably
because I used to own one back in California. Con-
necting with one of the kindest humans, Casey God-
love, makes PlantShed extra special. I'll never forget
when he reached out on Instagram and asked me to
illustrate all the PlantShed shop exteriors. His belief
in me changed how I saw myself and my art. Thanks
to Casey, I could finally call myself an artist.

Little Owl, 90 Bedford Street
Opposite: Abingdon Square Greenmarket, Hudson Street at
West 12th Street and 8th Avenue

81

Via Carota, 51 Grove Street

Now, let's stroll down Grove Street and West 7th, where decisions hang in the air like a tantalizing aroma. Via Carota beckons with its clams, clams, clams (undeniably irresistible). The scent of the sea drifts through the air, and you find yourself surrendering to the allure of those yummy clams.

The Stonewall Inn, 53 Christopher Street
Opposite: Cubbyhole, 281 West 12th Street

For me, the official start of summer is the city's Pride Parade. Shops and homes decked out in the spirit of happiness and togetherness make the West Village come alive. Walking through the Village, capturing signs, flags, and floral displays with the rainbow theme, I truly enjoy the vibrant atmosphere of June. In 2021, I met Scotty Elyanow, a true gem who knows the ins and outs of the Village. Walking with him, I learned the stories behind almost every building in which I showed interest. Aside from his engaging stories, he's always greeted by passersby with hellos, catch-ups, and exclamations of "Heeey Scotty, where have you been?!" Scotty mentioned that once you live in the Village, it becomes your community and your family. Beyond his vast knowledge lie Scotty's warmth and dedication to serving the community. He's involved in planting seasonal florals at Christopher Park, and I remember him sharing a picture of planting tulip bulbs. When spring comes, I visit the park to see the tulips blooming, covering the ground with beauty. Even though I may not know many people in the city, those I do come to know are priceless individuals with hearts of gold.

Stonewall National Monument, 38–64 Christopher Street

787 Coffee, 131 East 7th Street
Opposite: Davey's Ice Cream, 309 East 9th Street

Shuka, 38 MacDougal Street

Shuka at 38 MacDougal Street takes you into the world of Chef Ayesha, a thrill-seeker with a pineapple updo! Her warmth and authenticity make every visit a priceless experience. And, oh, the hummus with puffy pita and the carrot, fennel, radish salad is a culinary masterpiece!

Eva Joan, 28 Jane Street

And who could forget the creative paradise of Eva Joan at 28 Jane Street?
From vintage finds to whimsical embroidery, it's a haven for those seeking
one-of-a-kind treasures. My yellow and white vintage dress is a testament to
the magical discoveries that await you on your walks.

As the last day of summer dawns, I bid farewell with mixed emotions. The longer days, cafe outings, and ice cream delights will be missed, but the anticipation of fall's embrace stirs excitement. Until next year, dear Summer, thank you for the joy, laughter, and the beautiful stories only found in this city.

Variety Coffee, 261 7th Avenue, and Rosecrans Florist & Café, 7 Greenwich Avenue

FALL

A season for the hopeless romantics.

Dear Fall,

There's something truly magical about watching the leaves on the trees transform as they paint the city's streets with a palette of fiery reds, warm oranges, and golden yellows. It's as if the urban landscape itself becomes a canvas filled with the most striking colors, filling me with a sense of wonder, like unwrapping a fresh box of crayons.

The embrace of a snug sweater against my skin sends shivers of contentment down my spine, transporting me to a world of pure, snuggly bliss. During this season, you'll often find me outdoors, like in the springtime when I eagerly await the blossoming of cherry trees. Each day, I venture out to capture the mesmerizing beauty of autumn. I look for fresh fall foliage in flower beds, admire the blooms adorning people's pots, and stand in silent awe beneath the trees, where birds sing their cheerful melodies. Perhaps you too have felt the same, or maybe I'm just a hopeless romantic and a fan of the old movies that have immortalized autumn in New York.

Over time, I've realized that I don't need a backyard or flower bed of my own. All I have to do is step outside my apartment and there's an abundance of luscious beauty just waiting for me to savor.

I take leisurely strolls to enjoy seeing the leaves scattered on the ground, and it feels like each one is waiting for me to walk on by with a soft, satisfying rhythm of *crunch, crunch, crunch* for my ears.

Among all the trees, the ginkgo trees hold a special place in my heart. I find myself obsessively waiting for their leaves to turn a golden yellow, almost sad to bid farewell to their foliage. To me, they are the most exquisite, resembling little golden fans, gracefully falling to the ground. They are my dear autumn companions.

There have been days when I've waited and watched, sometimes for fifteen minutes, just to witness a single ginkgo leaf gently fall to the ground. You see, they say that when you see a ginkgo leaf fall, you can make a wish and it will come true. I remember a particular fall day in 2022 when I took a stroll along West 11th Street. Suddenly, I found myself standing beneath a ginkgo tree, surrounded by a shower of its leaves. It was as though I'd won the lottery! Of course, I made a wish. How could I not? I had waited all season (heck, all year!) for that moment and once again, my beloved city did not disappoint, gifting me with hundreds of golden leaves to behold.

In that instant, I felt immersed in a sea of gold, a world all my own, isolated from the urban chaos. I heard nothing but the joy and exuberance in my heart as the leaves continued their graceful descent, with one falling on my outstretched hand as I tried to capture its beauty. Such are life's little joys: effortless, pure, and in that moment, all mine to cherish.

Autumn in New York serves as a wake-up call to a season brimming with abundance, gratitude, and appreciation. The joy is on display as pumpkins adorn every corner, from the neighborhood bodegas to brownstones decorated with gourds and the occasional friendly ghost or goblin. Did I mention that I love Halloween? It's as though each year I'm transformed into a child once more.

With the arrival of October, I begin counting the days, wondering which neighbors will be the first to trick out their homes, eagerly anticipating the most creative displays. And until they start decorating, I always think, *Come on, folks, time's a-ticking!*

I've often wondered why I hold such affection for this particular season. Is it the relief from the sweltering summer heat, the feeling of inhabiting a romantic novel or movie, or is it merely because I cannot help but love it? It's all of these and more. It's as if the city itself whispers, "I'm here to offer a warm embrace and a bouquet of golden hues." How could one not fall in love with that?

I notice that fall also represents a season of letting go. Although our eyes see abundance, it's also a time to say goodbye. I didn't really notice that until writing this book. It hit me that soon the trees will be bare, getting ready to sleep through the winter months. This revelation made me think of my two boys, and how I remember those bittersweet moments of letting them go, sending them off to school for the first time, their little hands falling away from mine as they toddled to a whole new world, telling myself that I had to let them grow into their own lives. It gave me a feeling like there's a growing hole in my heart—something only a parent could understand.

So yes, there is a bit of sadness when this season ends. But the beauty embedded in our memories gives us the hope of seeing what's in store next.

Let's step into the spellbinding world of autumn together, where every leaf is a tiny, colorful miracle waiting to be caught! Can we hold hands and dash outside, giggling as we catch those leaves mid-fall, or perhaps stomp on them until the crisp crunching rhythm makes us dance with delight? Embracing the fall season is a cherished ritual in my city life. I'm practically bursting with excitement, skipping, jumping, and collecting leaves, indulging in every autumn craving.

West 4th Street

Corner Bistro, 331 West 4th Street
Opposite: Jackson Square, 8th Avenue and Greenwich Avenue

For months, I've been captivated by this charming home on Bank Street. It's not the home itself that caught my attention, but the lovely soul residing there along with her canine companion. One day, summoning my courage, I found myself sitting across the way on a bench at Waverly Inn. Crossing the street, I introduced myself, and that's when I had the pleasure of meeting Jenny and her irresistibly sweet dog, Buddy. Jenny's beautiful smile and warm eyes instantly made me feel at home.

We exchanged greetings and introductions but quickly got to into conversations about her knitting. Jenny loves sitting on her stoop with Buddy, crafting potholders with nimble fingers. She shared that when she was a child her dad taught her the art of knitting, and she used to knit on long drives with him. Pointing to a tree in front of her home, she mentioned, "I planted this tree over 38 years ago." And now that tree has grown into a majestic presence. Listening to her stories is an absolute delight! An hour and a half with her passes by in the blink of an eye.

Bank Street

The Old Yew Plant Shop, 1 Horatio Street

The Old Yew Plant Shop at 1 Horatio Street stole my heart when it first opened. Their topiaries are adorable, and the lush greenery in their backyard is a peaceful oasis. Despite my inability to keep plants alive, I visit just to say hello and get lost in my thoughts while hearing the water trickling down.

Fellini Coffee, 174 7th Avenue South

Fellini Coffee at 174 7th Avenue is the tiniest cafe in the West Village, and it's a pure delight. A new favorite on my list, its adorable charm captivates me, making each visit a joy.

L'Appartement 4F, 115 Montague Street, Brooklyn
Opposite: Cursive Home, 543 Hudson Street

John Derian Company, 6 East 2nd Street

John Derian Company at 6 East 2nd Street is a charming shop that defies description. I can literally spend hours here just looking at everything. It's so special that I felt too timid to enter for the first time because it's like nothing I've ever seen. The shop includes works of art by artists from all over the world. From a single crepe paper floral to beautiful chandeliers, each item is selected for its uniqueness and beauty. When I take a little field trip to this shop, all my senses are satisfied.

Joe Coffee Company, 141 Waverly Place

Buvette, 42 Grove Street

On a beautiful day in June, I was exploring New York and stumbled upon a neighborhood I had no knowledge of beforehand. I was on Bleecker Street and looked to my right to see a charming cafe. Craving coffee on this beautiful afternoon, I found my heart tickled by the exterior of this cafe. Upon entering Buvette, I was transported to another world. It wasn't New York, but a warm, quaint establishment in Paris. The clink of dishes, the hum of conversations, and the delicious smells were overwhelmingly delightful. I didn't know what to do; I was so mesmerized. Given the window seat, I couldn't stop looking around. My senses were on overload, and it honestly felt like a first love experience. Sitting there with my coffee, I said to myself, "One day, I'll live in this neighborhood," even though I still didn't even know which neighborhood I was in. And I didn't care. All I wanted was to live close to this wonderful cafe. Fast forward to now: Here I am, in the West Village, writing this book from my apartment, not far from Buvette. A dream that started from an accidental discovery. In early 2023, I had the opportunity to meet Chef Jody Williams of Buvette, and I have to admit, I was starstruck!

Buvette, 42 Grove Street

I Sodi, 314 Bleecker Street
Opposite: Grove Street Court

Let me paint you a picture of a home on West 4th Street, a constant source of inspiration, a real-life daydream. With each passing season and special day, this home is a canvas for my artistic musings. Whether adorned with decorations or standing in all its natural beauty, the townhouse is always a dose of inspiration. I make it a point to stroll down West 4th Street just to witness the ever-changing decor—I've even wandered by when they're in the middle of decorating. It's like peeking behind the curtain of a performance about to unfold. A visual spectacle, like a watercolor painting cascading out of the front door. Grateful doesn't quite cover it; I'm blessed to be a part of this neighborhood and community. Each day brings hidden surprises that never fail to tickle my heart. And to know that Susie, the owner of this dream home, is happy to be part of my book? Well, that's just the cherry on top of it all.

West 4th Street between Bank and West 12th Street

Charles Street and Bleecker Street
Opposite: Sex and the City home, Perry Street

Corner of Grove Street and Bedford Street
Opposite: Emmett's on Grove, 39 Grove Street

Sevilla, 62 Charles Street
Opposite: Té Company, 163 West 10th Street

This is a cherished spot in my illustrations, adopted in honor of my sweet Mollie. She wasn't just a pet; she was my best friend, my sidekick, my four-legged daughter. When my boys asked me me who I loved most, with a beaming smile, I'd always answer, "Mollie." Mollie knew me inside-out. She never asked for anything more than to love me unconditionally. After Mollie passed, while still in San Francisco, I adopted this park bench. It became a vessel for memories of Mollie, a piece of my future rather than my past. I knew that one day, I'd move to New York, leaving behind the home Mollie and I shared. So, I placed memories of her on this bench for the future—a destination to visit, to be reminded that love, cuddles, and plenty of snuggles live on. The engraving says it all: "When you use this bench, know that you're loved, cuddled, cherished, and receiving plenty of snuggles."

Washington Square Park

Corner of Perry Street and Bleecker Street
Opposite: Kobrick Coffee Co., 24 9th Avenue

Fishs Eddy, 889 Broadway

Hold on tight, because I'm about to describe the sheer delight that is Fishs Eddy at 889 Broadway! This oh-so-fun shop is a treasure trove for all things: dishes, cups, art, and more. Picture one of the most creative shops you've ever seen, that's practically bursting with inspiration. The team there are a bunch of artistic wizards building the most creative displays. And if, by chance, you catch Julie the owner there, now that's a treat! She's adorable, friendly, and the queen of great videos on her shop's Instagram page. Trust me, once you've experienced Fishs Eddy, you won't be tempted to go elsewhere for your dishware—it's a true one-stop shop.

Délice & Sarrasin, 178 West Houston Street
Opposite: The Commerce Inn, 50 Commerce Street

Bidding farewell to you, dear Fall, is the hardest part. Your beauty, with every color and cozy moment, has nourished my soul. From twirling in the midst of fallen leaves to the joyous stomping on the streets, you've been a continuous source of fun. Every year, your season seems the shortest and quickest, and I think because I love you so much, I never want you to go away. So, with a sigh, I say goodbye when all the leaves are gone. But I'm already counting down the days until I can welcome you back into my life. And in the meantime, I've got the magic of winter to enjoy . . .

WINTER

Snow in the city is pure magic.

Dear Winter,

You're officially here, and let me tell you, I'm positively thrilled! You might be wondering why I'm so excited about winter, and I've got a few reasons up my cozy, layered sleeves. You see, I'm from California, where to catch a glimpse snow there I would have to head to the mountains. But here in New York, the snow comes to me—I can open my window, stick my head and hands out, and catch those delicate snowflakes. When I step outside, I'm greeted by fluffy white snow—and yes, I know all about the mush and slush, but bear with me as I share my take on the winter wonderland in a city that graciously offers me all four seasons!

Winter in New York is a lot like that feeling I used to have as a child while waiting in line for an ice cream cone at the ice cream shop. You inch closer and closer to your treat, and the anticipation and excitement keep building. I find myself checking the weather app on my phone often, eagerly looking for signs of snow. My first snow experience in New York is etched in my memory. It was during a Nor'easter back in 2022. I think I was the only one in the neighborhood jumping with excitement, absolutely over the moon about the extraordinary snowfall! Sure, it was bone-chillingly cold, but I was determined to venture out and embrace the fresh snow.

Before coming to New York, I'd only seen snow on TV, in magazines, and in Google image searches. So my longing for snow runs deep in my soul. I've always daydreamed about a white Christmas, a real one, and the idea of building a snowman right outside my front door is simply mind-blowing. Seeing the city cloaked in a glistening white coat is pure magic. People bundle up in their warmest coats, scarves, and mittens and they hurry through the streets, their breath creating little puffs of steam in the chilly air. The city lights sparkle like stars in the night sky. I'm so filled with joy that I want to embrace every single moment of the winter season!

Now, I'm sure you're thinking, *Is she a bit nuts?* After days of snow, the yucky parts of winter are hard to miss: the black ice, the less-than-fluffy brown slush, all so "not-a-snow-cone." It's not that I don't see the mess or feel the achy, chilling cold. And some days, even the simplest errand like a grocery run feels like a major effort. Often, I hesitate to go out, having to bundle up in layers upon heavy layers where I'll be waddling under the weight of my clothing. I feel all of that. But, despite the cold and its challenges, there's something truly wonderful about winter in New York.

I love the evenings when I can see though people's windows into their warm, beautifully lit homes. You catch a glimpse of a homeowner going about their day and keeping warm inside their cozy apartment. I remember seeing a woman sitting by the window having what looked to be a warm drink, wearing a beanie while inside her home. It was cold and that "home hat" was an extra layer of warmth for her. That moment took me back in time to my four-foot-eleven-inch grandmother who used to wear a beanie on winter days in the house. Being a child, I thought it was strange that she would be wearing a hat inside, but I came to understand that her aging body was sensitive to the cold. She'd wear a thick sweater-coat that eventually I wanted to wear because it felt like a warm hug from my grandma. She gave me her coat and I wore it to school in the winter months to feel her right next to me, hugging me. I actually felt a tug in my heart on that evening walk in my neighborhood.

Prince Street

Guess who's here? It's you, Winter, my chilly companion! I can't help but notice your arrival when I find myself piling on layers and grabbing thermals just to step out. You always bring that thrill down my spine, and I eagerly await your magical touch as you blanket the city like meringue on a tart. No matter how frosty you get, you have this knack for pulling me out, taking my hand, and leading me to fun! Our little adventures together are my favorite, and I hope you catch me whispering my happiness to you. Thanks for the snowy surprise outside my door, the perfect canvas for our winter escapades. I'm all set. Let's play!

Jackson Square

Staple Street

Opposite: Corner of Horatio Street and Greenwich Avenue

Bubby's, 120 Hudson Street

I confess, I'm a bit infatuated with the little black-and-white cow standing guard outside Bubby's in Tribeca, and I snap a photo of it every time I pop by for a homemade pie or a pile of pancakes for brunch.

Corner of West 4th and West 11th

It's the homes, whether layered brick or beautiful brownstones, that make the West Village truly special. It's like living in a backdrop for classic movies, and their enduring charm is unmatched.

145

DEAR NEW YORK, I LOVE YOU

Bleecker Street

Walking along Bleecker Street on a winter day, imagine my surprise finding a snow-covered cab! It felt like it was calling out for a snowy message, and I couldn't resist. Scribbling, "I love NY xo" in the snow was a moment of pure silly fun, a memory that's etched in my New York journey.

Daddies, 450 Hudson Street
Opposite: Rockefeller Center, 45 Rockefeller Plaza

Inscope Arch, Central Park

Tenement Museum, 103 Orchard Street

151

Haar & Co. Barbershop, 45 Christopher Street
Opposite: Greenwich Letterpress, 15 Christopher Street

It was a cold winter day. I had just returned from a long walk of exploring the city only to realize how hungry I was. The first thing that popped into my mind was a warm bowl of matzah ball soup. Immediately, I thought of Russ & Daughters Cafe on Orchard Street. I had never been there before and was excited to finally dine in one of the city's most beloved establishments. The coziness of the cafe is a throwback to a time when diners were the place to be. Dishes clank and silverware echoes throughout the restaurant, and there's a constant buzz of people talking and enjoying their meals. I, too, was a part of this mix and felt so excited.

After a perfect meal of matzah ball soup, the waitress gave me my check. As I looked down at the black tray with my bill, I saw something that I haven't seen since I was 13 years old: a coffee candy called Hopjes. It's a hard candy that honestly sings in your mouth; the same candy my grandfather would always carry in his pocket. It was his favorite. The last time I had seen this candy was the year my grandfather passed.

This unexpected candy encounter at Russ & Daughters brought back a beautiful memory of my grandfather. In that moment, I saw him pulling out the candy from his pocket to give me one as a treat for sitting still. I saw his gentle smile as he expressed how proud he was of me. And seeing his endearing and gentle eyes in my mind brought happy tears. Thank you, Russ & Daughters Cafe, for bringing my grandfather back to me once again so I could feel his love.

Russ & Daughters Cafe, 127 Orchard Street

La Bonbonniere, 28 8th Avenue

Since I moved to New York, Marina and Gus at La Bonbonniere have been like family. Their warm welcome and comforting breakfasts are a piece of home. Marina's heart of gold and Gus's gem-like personality make La Bonbonniere a special place. They're like the mom and dad of the West Village.

Bien Cuit, 120 Smith Street, Brooklyn
Opposite: Rosecrans Florist & Cafe, 7 Greenwich Avenue

Historic 1800s carriage house, 78 Irving Place
Opposite: The March Hare, 321 East 9th Street

Grand Central Terminal
Opposite: Subway in Queens

DEAR NEW YORK, I LOVE YOU

12 Chairs Cafe, 56 MacDougal Street
Opposite: Muse Shop, 605 Hudson Street

C.O. Bigelow Chemists, 414 6th Avenue
Opposite: McNulty's Tea & Coffee, 109 Christopher Street

Café Grumpy, 13 Essex Street
Opposite: Chelsea Market, 75 9th Avenue

You might think I'm a bit crazy, and for a moment, I thought so too for actively wanting to play in the snow during my first Nor'easter experience! It was a dream come true, seeing so much snow. When I checked my weather app, it showed that the temperature had dropped to 18°F. So I bundled up in layers, grabbed my trusted HotHands hand warmers, and marched out to experience the snow. The streets were quiet, with only a few people around. I could literally hear my own footsteps as I walked through the snowy field. My glasses fogged up, my toes started freezing, and I realized, *Wow, this is really cold!* But the excitement of exploring the neighborhood in the snow kept me going until I couldn't go any further. Hailing a cab to warm up and head home was the perfect finale!

The Nor'easter of 2022

And finally, goodbye Winter. Let's find a cozy spot on a stoop to bid farewell to the last day of winter. Today, I'm saying goodbye to frosted windows, fluffy snow, and the not-so-pretty slush. The bone-chilling temperatures and gusty winds will soon be a memory. Despite your temperament, I have a special fondness for you, especially during the holidays. Until we meet again, goodbye for now.

Sixteen Mill Bakeshop, 552 Union Street, Brooklyn

Acknowledgments

To my community, thank you for embracing my art, opening your hearts, and adding your own magic to these pages.

A special thank you to Nikki Kule, Max Poglia, and the Floratorium team—you've inspired me so deeply with your artistry.

Thank you to Andrew, Annie, Daniel, and David for your unwavering love.

Thank you to Leigh, my wonderful agent who set me on this amazing journey, and to the team at Countryman Press—Emma, Ann, Allison, Sarah, Jess, Devon, Sean, Roxanne, Ken, Anika, Maya, Zachary, Devorah, and Isabel—for bringing my book to life!

To Tom, your support is treasured and you are such a gem!

To my New York doctors—Dr. Jaime Royal, Dr. Gwendolyn Reeve, Dr. Suzette Gerardi, Dr. Stephanie Chang, Dr. Elaine Shum, Dr. Valerie Lyon, Dr. Inga Zilberstein, Dr. Anne Bass, Dr. Jessica Starr, and Dr. Jennifer Bonheur—I'm so grateful to be under your care.

To Surfin, Mike, Steve, Daynion, Eric, Johnny, Abdul, Pablo, Robert, Marcos, Ray, Richard, Jose, and sweet Martha—you hold a special place in my heart as my first New York family!

And, finally, to my darling Mollie. You were my constant companion, never leaving me alone in my creative journey. And now, here it is, my first book. I love and miss you dearly, sweet girl.

Dear Readers,

Thank you for unwrapping the magic within these pages. What began as a healing process has led me to the creation of my first book, and every one of you played a vital role in this transformative journey, encouraging me to persist and refine my artistic skills. Life is full of mysteries, and as one door closes, another opens—yes, even the doggie doors!

To my young readers, may this book kindle the flame of your dreams. Never surrender to the challenges. I, with no education past high school, hurdled countless obstacles. Persevere, little ones—nurture beauty in your hearts, and one day you'll witness that beauty materialize. Live in the realm of imagination for a brighter tomorrow. Dwell in a space filled with love and laughter and embrace each moment with grace.

To my ageless readers, I walk hand-in-hand with you. Life has dealt us highs and lows, heartbreaks, losses, and failures. Yet, we forge ahead, overcoming the obstacles thrown our way. The heartbreaks that once felt insurmountable, the grief of losing loved ones, and the trials that fueled our strength—I stand beside you on these journeys. May we continue to dream, for we are never too old or mature to wish upon that star. Let us persist as the architects of our hopes and dreams coming true.

To my seasoned readers, I turn to you for guidance and inspiration. Your gift of insight is a beacon of light. It's that wisdom I aim to acquire. Sometimes I still feel lost, but I look to you to reassure myself that everything will be fine. I envision the day I meet my 98-year-old self, sitting on Mollie's Bench at the park, feeling the autumn breeze on my cheeks, and hearing you say, "Your dream brought you to this moment, and I've believed in you since the day you were born."

With heartfelt gratitude,
Ria